Eagle Eyes:
A Collection of True Hunting Stories

Todd E. Miller

Introduction

Before we begin allow me to introduce myself, my name is Todd E. Miller. Typically speaking I'm a hunter not a writer. However over the years I have had many wonderful experiences in the woods in which I feel the need to share with my fellow American outdoors-men. I hope that many of you can enjoy and relate to these stories as we all pass down the tradition of hunting to future generations.

I began hunting when I was seventeen years old and I shot my first deer that year. The joy I felt from my accomplishment was as overwhelming as the vastness of the woodland in which I shot him. It was a true milestone in my life as a hunter. In the years since I have hunted a 320 pound black bear and a 60 pound coyote (as well as several other deer); both with my 30-30 Winchester Model '94. Also in my arsenal of artillery is a 30-06, a 270, a

243, a 12 gauge, a 357, and a 44. One thing that I have found to be important overtime is diversity in arms. Don't get me wrong, I don't mean to boast, I'm just a man who loves to hunt.

The stories you are about to read, however unique, aren't fictitious but true stories of my experiences as a hunter. However some parts of this book may take the shape of a journal of my current hunting endeavors. I hope you enjoy reading about them as much as I enjoyed the journey of living them. And all it took to have such fun was a love to hunt, the right gun, and of course the eyes of an eagle.

Chapter 1

There are some hunting trips you just never forget, as was the case on this trip with my dad and cousin. We had been out in the woods enjoying the day as we often do; there was a deer within range. I lined up my cross-hairs on his chest (always aim for the heart when deer hunting). I steadied myself and squeezed the trigger, *'Bang!'* The deer dropped dead without the usual kick of his hind legs and the run that follows. The three of us worked our way over to where the bullet hit home; to our surprise there was not one but two dead deer. The bullet had ripped straight through the parallel duo, talk about two for one! That was one shot I couldn't have made if I tried.

Chapter 2

One of my most interesting (although my saddest) hunting experiences was the one of two boys I met in the woods. Once again I was out hunting with my dad. We had temporarily split up to cover more ground. As we went our separate ways I came across two kids who were hauling a deer by means of a rope tied around its neck. The deer had been shot and wounded but it was still alive.

"What are you two doing?" I asked.

"We're taking the deer to grandpa," they replied. "He's a doctor; he can help pull the bullet out."

I found my dad and we offered to help take the deer to their grandfather. When we arrived the grandfather came out of the house and examined the deer.

"This deer has lost too much blood," the old man said.

I had no choice but to put to put the deer out of its misery. One of the kids grabbed me by the leg.

"Please mister, please don't shoot the deer," he said. But the grandfather took them inside the house so they wouldn't have to watch.

"I'm sorry I have to do this," I said as they went inside. "But I don't want the deer to suffer."

I pulled out my 357 and shot the deer. That was the hardest shot I've ever had to make in my life.

Chapter 3

Let's take a moment to talk about long range shooting. In the past I have made shots varying from 300 to 400 yards. The best shot that I've been able to accomplish was a 400 yard shot with my 30-06 Winchester Model '70. Despite this I still wish I could shoot with the accuracy of Charles Hancock who was, in my opinion, the best shot ever.

When it comes to learning how to hunt, I have learned a lot from an unexpected place; my cat Penguilla. My mother found her as a stray, fed her, and took her in. The cat was black and white so my mother came up with the name Penguilla because she had the colors of a penguin. Over the years I have watched her hunt mice, chipmunks, and birds. The one thing I have noticed is that, through her animal instinct, she wouldn't attack immediately rather she would let her prey come in close to her before going in for the kill. I have learned that this is the best way to hunt no matter whether you're hunting deer, turkey, bear, or whatever. Let them come to you by calling them in, don't go to them. It just goes to show how smart animals can be when it comes to survival. We can learn a lot from them as I have learned a lot from Penguilla. I have come to love that cat as a member of the family.

Chapter 4

The best shot that I have ever made involved a coyote I hunted that was on the run. When I saw the coyote I told my dad that I would shoot the coyote in the back of the head and make the bullet come out of his eye. Believe it or not, that is exactly what I managed to do. Now the coyote has two fake eyes, one replacing the shot eye and the other replacing his good eye, and he stands as my trophy.

Chapter 5

There was one day when again I was out hunting with my dad and we had to take shelter in the middle of a storm. We went into the old barn on the property we were given permission to hunt on in order to stay warm. It was starting to get dark out and our day was almost at an end when we saw a deer out in the field.

"If you're going to shoot its now or never," my dad said.

I took the shot and hit the deer in the head, usually I would aim for the heart as I've said but I had to improvise, and the deer dropped dead.

Chapter 6

One of the funniest things that I have seen in the woods happened when I came upon a field of sleeping deer. I told my dad that I was going to shoot one of them and I took my shot. The funny part was the deer never bucked when I shot him, he just kept sleeping there and so did the rest of them. We waited and watched for awhile but they just kept sleeping. Finally we went out into the field to retrieve the deer I killed and when we did the rest of them suddenly woke up and ran for it. As for the deer I shot, at least he went peacefully; after all he slept through the whole thing.

Chapter 7

I have been hunting for a long time now, ever since I was a young teenager, and I have noticed as time goes on that there is more and more hunting pressure. There are more ATV's and other sport vehicles out in the country these days which scares away the animals. There are more posted signs on farmland then there used to be and become a lot harder to find land to hunt on. Farmland is the best place to hunt because animals like to feed on the crops but open farmland is becoming scarce. You can ask for permission to hunt on a person's land but it's becoming more common for people to reject you out of the fear of being sued. With the economy as bad as it is some people would sue over the smallest thing just because they need the money and a smart farmer wouldn't want to take that risk. There is always state land but that's never as good as farmland because you hardly ever find the animal you're hunting. Personally I think that there should be more land available for hunters so that we can pass the tradition on to future generations.

Chapter 8

There has been a lot of debate in recent years about opening up a second deer season because the deer are overpopulated. However it said that the deer are overpopulated every year and no action is ever actually taken. What people fail to consider is the number of deer that are hit by cars and killed off by predators, these factors take a major toll on their population. I feel that a second deer season would actually make the deer under populated. While I enjoy deer hunting I don't believe that a second deer season is needed.

Chapter 9

I have spent a lot of time so far talking about deer hunting but I would like to take a moment to talk about turkey hunting. I love to hunt turkey just about as much as I love to hunt deer and while they are both a challenge they are a challenge in different ways. For instance turkeys have excellent eye sight and can see a hunter from miles away. When you hunt deer you are supposed to wear hunter-orange so other hunters can see you and don't shoot you by accident. Supposedly deer can't see the orange (although sometimes I wonder) but turkey can. Therefore when you hunt turkey you must dress only in camouflage to successfully hide yourself and sometimes that doesn't even work. Also turkeys are obviously a lot smaller than deer and thusly a smaller target. But despite how hard it is to hunt turkey I still love the challenge.

Chapter 10

Recently I have been after this silver fox that I came across in the woods. When I saw him he poked his head out of some brush but I couldn't get a clear shot and he ran off. I've been trying to call in ever since using different calls such as rapid-distress calls. I will continue to look for him until the season ends and I will be looking forward to the upcoming spring turkey season.

Chapter 11

I would like to take a moment to explain something that I am currently doing that is actually not hunting related to add to this memoir. I am currently getting prepared for a test to become a security guard and hopefully that goes well. I will try to keep this book updated as time goes on.

Chapter 12

Yesterday my dad bought a new turkey call and he said that he wanted to try it out. We went out to woods just to do some pre-turkey season calling and we heard a gobbler. My dad called again but the gobbler didn't respond this time. Moments later a large coyote emerged from the brush right in front of us and ran off! It was like something you would see on television.

Chapter 13

The other day I was at the corner store in my hometown and I was talking to Dave, the store's owner. This old man came in and started talking to us about his favorite spot for trout fishing in upstate New York. He was upset that there have been a lot of tiger muskies let loose in the water which was eating off all the other fish such as trout and perch. He said he was upset with the way New York State was handling things, something I have heard a lot lately from different people.

Chapter 14

I was in a café the other day and was talking to some other hunters. I learned something about turkey hunting from an old timer. He told me that the key is to do more flapping. He said I need to make some yips then go to flapping; do yips and yelps then go back to flapping and make a pattern out of it. It sounded like good advice and I'm definitely going to give it a try.

Chapter 15

It is now coyote season, I haven't been out yet but I have seen some big coyotes near where I live. I hope to get one and if I do I will be sure to mention it later on in this book.

Chapter 16

So far I haven't been out coyote hunting as much as I would like. However I have been to a gun auction that was quite interesting. I didn't buy anything but they had a lot of military equipment on display. But I still have to get out coyote hunting because turkey season is on its way. I have a lot of new things I need to try out when I go turkey hunting including new turkey decoys. I want to see if the new decoys will work better than my old ones. I will probably talk more about that later in this book.

Chapter 17

I tried out the decoys on this year's spring turkey. They brought in a lot of hens and Jakes but there weren't any Toms which is what I was hoping for. I didn't shoot anything but I was pleased to see the hens and Jakes. Fall is right around the corner and we'll see what the fall season brings here in New York. Fishing season is also coming up so I'll probably do some fishing. I like to fish for bass, pike, and walleye but I always let them go, catch and release. Fishing is just something I like to do for fun until hunting season opens up again.

Chapter 18

I just got a ground blind that I'm going to use this season. I have hunted from a tree-stand and I have still-hunted but I have never hunted from a ground blind so I'm very excited about this new opportunity. However I have to wait until hunting season opens up again. In the meantime I will continue fishing. I have been out twice already and have caught a little bass but nothing spectacular. Before long deer season and turkey season will roll around and I'm going to use my new ground blind for both.

I bought the ground blind from an outdoors-man shop the other day with my dad. I haven't actually set it up in the woods yet but we did get to see it all set up. It took longer than five minutes to set it up like they tell you on television but its good and I look forward to using it on a hunt.

Chapter 19

I've been out turkey hunting a lot recently but I haven't had any luck. I've heard stories from other hunters who have seen some but I've been hunting in a new spot that hasn't had too many. I did see some Toms and I tried to call them in but they were with hens and I couldn't break them apart well enough to get a clear shot. I tried to sneak up on them as well but that didn't work either.

Deer season opens this Saturday the 18th and I'm excited about that. I never did use the ground blind for fall turkey but I will use it for deer season. I will be going out with my dad and if we get anything I'll be sure to mention it in this book.

Chapter 20

I went out deer hunting with my dad but we didn't get anything. My dad had a shot at a doe that was running pretty fast but he missed, it was a hard shot for a 70 year old man to make. I do know a spot where there is a nice buck though and I'm going to go out later this afternoon and try to find him. I've been studying his habits like when he comes out and when he doesn't. Hopefully today will be the day it pays off.

Chapter 21

Well deer season is now over and I didn't get anything. However I did get a shot at a nice buck and the strangest thing happened. I made a back of the head shot and the bullet actually ricocheted off the deer's head. The deer dropped to the ground unconscious and I thought I killed it but when I walked up to it and kicked him he jumped up and ran away. I was pretty bummed out about it but sometimes strange things like that happen when you're in the woods.

Spring turkey season is on its way again but hopefully I can get out hunting coyote and foxes first. I plan on using my '22 Jett pistol for that which I have put a scope on. I just have to find the right box of bullet heads for that and then I can let you know more later on.

Chapter 22

I took my pistol out the other to day so I could sight it in. I still don't have it exactly where I want it, but I'm working on it. I've been using '22 long rifles lately but I still want to get heads for the '22 Jett because pretty soon I want do some fox and coyote hunting with my friend. We haven't been out yet, but we're planning on it.

Chapter 23

I finally got out fox and coyote hunting but I haven't shot anything yet. I just got a box of heads that I'm going to use for my '22 Jett. However I have been using my '22 long rifle and my handgun but I haven't had a shot with those either. I have seen some though but I couldn't get a good clean shot.

Chapter 24

I feel like I should say a few words about a good friend of mine who recently passed away named Chuck Bliss. Like me, Chuck was a hunter and fisherman. I would just like to say that I will miss hunting and fishing with Chuck and that he will be greatly missed.

Chapter 25

I have been out coyote hunting recently but I haven't had any luck so far. I have been working on a Smith & Wesson handgun (.22 Jett) that I want to use to shoot a coyote. However I have to get a new tap for it and put the scope back on it.

Chapter 26

I didn't get any coyotes with my .22 handgun, unfortunately. I had some problems with the gun and I will have to work on it all over again. I didn't plan on doing so but after careful consideration I have changed my mind. After all, I enjoy working on guns almost as much as I enjoy hunting. I will keep you updated on the matter.

Chapter 27

Spring turkey season is rapidly approaching here in Upstate New York and I am looking forward to trying out my ground blind. It is the same blind that I use during deer season and it is a quality product so I am hoping that I will see some satisfying results this year. I have been watching a group of turkey for some time now, trying to find a pattern in their daily routine and such. I've been trying out different calls so maybe they will help. I might do some fishing this year as trout season has just opened up so I might attempt to get one. I also heard on the news that there have been a lot of bobcat sightings so I would like to get a shot at one of them. If I have any luck I will be sure to record it in this book.

Chapter 28

Spring turkey season has just ended and I unfortunately did not get anything. I was able to call in a nice tom and I took a shot but misfired. Hopefully I will have better luck next year.

Chapter 29

I do not want to say too much about my personal life outside of the hunting world but I do want to mention at least one more thing. I have just found out that my dad will be completely blind someday, within two years the doctor said. It hit me hard to hear that because my dad has been my hunting partner ever since I was a kid and knowing that someday soon he won't be able to hunt at all is hard for the both of us. But if I have learned one thing from this experience it is how fast life passes by and how quickly medical complications can take control of your life. My advice to everybody reading this book is to enjoy every minute you have and to cherish the time you have with your loved ones. Don't waste your time by being a miserable cynic but enjoy life and love one another, we are all God's children.

Chapter 30

Fall turkey season is coming up and deer season shortly after that, in November. I am hopeful of getting a tom and as always I will keep you updated…

Chapter 31

I did get a tom this turkey season but deer season has started and my buddy Dave and I have killed a six point buck that weighed in at 160 lbs. I shot him once and Dave shot him twice and we were finally able to drag him out of the woods. There is still a nicer buck out there, a ten or eleven point, which we would like to get. We're going back out on Tuesday to rattle him in and I think if we work together we might stand a chance. Dave is an excellent hunter and a good friend and I sure hope that we go on more hunts together in the future.

Chapter 32

The other day something rather strange happened to me. I was out coyote hunting with a decoy and a blower that I use that sounds like a wounded rabbit. Instead an ugly possum with sharp teeth and claws came out and stole the decoy; he tried to run away with it into the woods. I shot him instead. I didn't get a coyote that day but I guess it's better to get a possum than nothing at all.

Chapter 33

Today I was out fishing with my friend Dave and I caught the biggest bass I have ever caught in my life. I know I wasn't going to put many fishing stories in here but this one I feel I should tell. I caught the bass with a lure and got him up to the shore. The line broke and he got away, taking the lure with him. It was a shame that I lost him but I'm hoping to try to catch him again someday.

Chapter 34

A few days ago I was out turkey hunting with Dave, my dad, and my nephew. The day was coming to a close, we were getting ready to leave, and we hadn't turkey. As we were loading up the car we heard a gobble that was *really* close so my nephew and I went into the woods to see if we could get any while Dave and my dad waited in the car. I was in the lead but my nephew saw them first. I was too far away for him to tell me where they were; if he spoke up it would have scared them away. He would have taken the shot himself but he was worried he might shoot me instead because the angle wasn't in his favor; I didn't realize this at the time. Finally I saw them and took a shot but it was too late, they were flying away and I missed. I asked my nephew why he didn't take a shot to which he responded:

"Well I had tom fever!"

On the ride home he told me what really happened. I'll never forget that trip and we all are still laughing about it.

Chapter 35

Deer season has just ended and it is now December 7th, 2008. I was able to get a doe this year with a 270, it was the first time I have used one. I have to say I was very pleased with the gun and I will definitely use it some more. I did have some disappointment this year though. I was able to hit a gorgeous 10-point buck, the most beautiful deer I have ever seen but some people came and took the deer before I could get to it. I called the game warden and they were fined but deer was never found. I hope that I will get a shot at another deer like that someday.

On a happier note, coyote season is coming up so I might get a chance to take down a coyote. A friend of mine asked me if I want to go on a muzzle-loader hunt with him. I'm not much of a muzzle-loader hunter but I'm considering doing that as well.

Chapter 36

I didn't get a chance to go on the muzzle-loader hunt, the season just went by too quickly and I got caught up in other things. However I did go on some coyote hunts and I think that a saw a silver-fox on one of them. It ran quickly and I saw it out of the corner of my eye and I didn't take a shot at him but it was a wonderful experience nonetheless.

Chapter 37

I would like to mention another fishing experience, if I may. On June 26th I caught a 10 pound large mouth bass in Silver Lake, New York. This one didn't break the line and get away like the last one. My father-in-law lives there and we go fishing in the lake when we visit sometimes. It was the largest bass I ever caught so it was a pretty exciting experience. Other than that turkey season is coming up and I will let you know how that turns out in the next chapter.

Chapter 38

Turkey season came and went and I didn't get anything. I did see some nice toms but I couldn't really get a shot. I do have some news that I would like to include in this book, it is a bit more of a personal matter. Our family cat Penguilla passed away the other day. She has been in our family for quite some time now and loosing her is like loosing a loved one. You don't realize how close a pet is to you until you loose them. She passed away under my mother's lilac bush where she is now buried. She will be greatly missed.

Chapter 39

I finally got my big buck this year on the first day of deer season (November 21st) while out hunting with my buddy Mike; he's an older gentleman who lives near me. The buck was a beautiful 8-pointer and he is at the taxidermist now. I wish Penguilla was still around to see it. I always told her that someday I would get the big buck with the horns on its head and the rest of the family always thought that was funny. Now I got the big buck and I wish she was still here. We all miss you Penguilla.

Chapter 40

Yesterday, May 7th, 2010, I was out spring turkey hunting and I got a beautiful turkey at last, a 19.3 pound tom with a 10 inch beard; magnificent colors, the biggest tom I have ever shot. He is at the taxidermy now; in fact it is the same taxidermy that is doing my deer. It's an expensive service but it will be worth it in the end. I am so happy about it and I had to put in my book before I finish writing it.

The day that I shot him I was sitting up against a tree, flapping and calling. I had decoys but I wasn't even using them at the time. The turkey approached from the left which took me by surprise. I was expecting him to approach from the right. I have been hunting this bird for about three years and he always outsmarted me. This time I got in a position where I could be back in the woods a little bit but still cover the field. This time I outsmarted him and took him down with my 20 gauge Winchester model 37.

Chapter 41

I have saved my favorite and best hunting story for last. Once while I was deer hunting I was trekking through the woods and my day was almost at a close. I saw a dark mass from my peripheral vision. I looked up and saw that it was a big black bear. The bear stood up on its hind legs and began to growl loudly. I only had two shots in my 30-30. I took my first shot and the bullet hit him in the chest but the bear wasn't even phased by it and appeared to be getting angrier. I took my second and final shot and the bullet hit right next to the first. The bear fell on all fours, staggered a bit, and fell over dead.

I went home and told my dad what had happened.

We went back into the woods and searched for the body. By the time we got back it was dark and we had to use flashlights to find him. Finally we came to the body and dad stood back with the gun.

"Kick him," he said. "If he growls, I'm shooting and running for the car."

I prodded the bear and it did not move. When we took it home before taking it to the taxidermy my nephew, who was young at the time, saw it and said: "Phew, tinky bear." We had it weighed in at 326lbs and turned into a bear rug. It was a hunting endeavor I will never forget.

Chapter 42

As I wrap up this book I would like to say a few words about my parents. As I said my father is having trouble with his eyesight and mother is also very sick, she has cancer which the doctor said has spread to her bones. I want more than anything to finish this book before anything happens to them. I want them to be proud. My parents have raised me since I was a child and have loved and cared for me to the fullest and it hurts to see them in such a state. I pray for them everyday.

I still get out hunting but it isn't the same as when I used to go out with my dad, my brother, and my uncle. Things have just changed a lot for me over the years. I still go out but it's mostly with friends or alone. I take my dad out but usually only once a year due to his eyesight and he's really upset by that because he doesn't want to give up hunting but he really can't anymore. Most of all he doesn't like people telling him that he can't. All in all I miss the old days but I'm glad that I have such wonderful memories to look back on and I want such memories to exist for generations to come.

Conclusion

I had once been asked an interesting question which was: "do you believe in reincarnation?" I replied: "no, not really."

However the man asked: "if you did come back as something else, what would it be?"

I thought about it for a moment and replied: "A bald headed eagle."

If I was an eagle I could soar through the clouds over mother earth, fly high above the waterfalls and streams, over the majestic mountains of the United States of America, and see everything with a birds eye view with my eagle eyes; it would be beautiful, it would be peaceful. My soul would have been fulfilled.

About the Author

Todd E. Miller was an American hunter and fisherman. Unfortunately, Todd passed away unexpectedly in February of 2015 of a sudden massive heart attack, he was 49 years old. This book has been compiled in his memory by his family from recordings he left behind on cassette. The publication of this book was one of his last wishes. We hope it is everything he dreamed it would be. RIP Todd, we love and miss you.